STRIPPING
My Fight to Find Me

A collection of poems

SUNITA MERRIMAN

BALBOA
PRESS
A DIVISION OF HAY HOUSE

Balboa Press books may be ordered through booksellers or by contacting:

Balboa Press
A Division of Hay House
1663 Liberty Drive
Bloomington, IN 47403
www.balboapress.com
1 (877) 407-4847

Because of the dynamic nature of the Internet, any web addresses or links contained in this book may have changed since publication and may no longer be valid. The views expressed in this work are solely those of the author and do not necessarily reflect the views of the publisher, and the publisher hereby disclaims any responsibility for them.

The author of this book does not dispense medical advice or prescribe the use of any technique as a form of treatment for physical, emotional, or medical problems without the advice of a physician, either directly or indirectly. The intent of the author is only to offer information of a general nature to help you in your quest for emotional and spiritual well-being. In the event you use any of the information in this book for yourself, which is your constitutional right, the author and the publisher assume no responsibility for your actions.

Certain stock imagery © Getty Images.

Printed in the United States of America.

ISBN: 978-1-9822-0021-3 (sc)
ISBN: 978-1-9822-0023-7 (hc)
ISBN: 978-1-9822-0022-0 (e)

Library of Congress Control Number: 2018903386

Balboa Press rev. date: 07/12/2018

Each poem is in honor of the brave souls who start the journey in search of their truth and of the beautiful souls who lovingly hold their hand along the way.

For
Daddy,
Tim,
Nina, and Simrin

Dedicated to
John Hans Rathauser

February 24, 2020

Dear Morgan,

Here's to Love!

Because what else is there
to talk about...

All the best on your
magical journey ahead,

Amita..

Poetry that translates the language and spirit of the
unconscious as it transforms pain and suffering into
hope.

Cache

I can only recall little things,
But I remember everything.

—Sunita Merriman

Contents

Epigraph

"Once you start to awaken, no one can ever claim you again for the old patterns. Now you realise how precious your time here is. You are no longer willing to squander your essence on undertakings that do not nourish your true self; your patience grows thin with tired talk and dead language. You see through the rosters of expectation which promise you safety and the confirmation of your outer identity. Now you are impatient for growth, willing to put yourself in the way of change. You want your work to become an expression of your gift. You want your relationship to voyage beyond the pallid frontiers to where the danger of transformation dwells. You want your God to be wild and to call you to where your destiny awaits."

—John O'Donohue

Permission to publish this passage provided by
the John O'Donohue Literary Estate
© 2018 by John O'Donohue. All rights reserved.

Preface

I was woefully unprepared for the most important love of my life.

This discovery, sadly, didn't come to me in the form of an epiphany but as an incidental finding as I sought help for an unease that had made its home in my mind for as far back as I could remember.

As I ventured into the underground world of my unconscious, I encountered locked doors, secret passages, and hidden rooms. Until my poems started to come to me, I didn't believe I had the keys to the mysterious secrets that lay deep inside me.

My words were like the lighthouse to the workings of my inner world. They guided me toward my buried past. They refused to give up on me when I felt I could no longer fight through the unbearable loneliness and pain of my memories. They cheered for me every time I had a breakthrough and gained insight. Sometimes they came to me in a torrent. Other times they made me anxiously wait for them to reveal themselves. But whenever they appeared, they brought me my truth.

My poems taught me that there is no truth without honesty and that honesty doesn't exist where there is no courage—and that for me to be courageous, I had to turn my back on shame. And strip.

I wrote these poems for myself.
I read them when I need to find solace and comfort.
I read them when I need to find the strength to go on.

I read them when I need to be inspired.
I read them when I need to be reminded that I am
much bigger than the fight I have had to fight.
I read them, so I always remember how brave I am.

These poems are my story.

My story is your story

Because I am you.

I hope my fight inspires you to find your own truth.
I wish you the most sacred of all loves, self-love.
Because you are worth it, you deserve it, and you are entitled to it.

Sincerely,
Sunita

Acknowledgments

Writing this book was a solitary journey. However, it's creation was not.

There are many more people than I could possibly mention here who have been a part of my healing process. I thank you with a grateful heart for walking with me when I was struggling and needed you.

I met up with my dear friend Maria at the Nat King Cole Bar in the St. Regis Hotel in Manhattan on March 11, 2016, to belatedly celebrate our birthdays. I read her a couple of my poems. That was it. She was adamant that I should publish them in a book. "There are so many people who need to hear your poems." Maria, I thank you for believing in the healing power of my words and in me. I love you.

Thank you to Pradeep, Dimple, and Linda, who listened to my work as I was writing it and trying to understand it. Your constant support and encouragement were invaluable to me and always gave me strength. You are some of the very special treasures in my life.

I earnestly appreciate all my friends and family who never complained to me about receiving texts with attachments of my poems at very unsocial hours as the poems came into creation. Thank you for your loving and encouraging feedback.

I honor my principal at Yadavindra Public School in Patiala, Panjab, India, the late H. N. Kashyap, as the person who ignited my love for poetry. He enthusiastically passed on his passion for the written word to me and encouraged me to pursue my love for writing as an expression of who I am.

John O' Donahue, the late poet, priest, scholar, and philosopher, held space for me at times when I felt I could barely breathe, let alone forge ahead with strength. The beauty and wisdom of his words and spirit consoled me and encouraged me to look beyond my moments of despair. Many thanks to his literary estate for granting me the permission to include my favorite passage by him in *Stripping: My Fight to Find Me.*

I am indebted to Dr. Habib Davanloo. His lifelong dedication to understanding and teaching others how the human unconscious can be successfully and predictably accessed for therapeutic relief is responsible for the healing of my brain. The damage I suffered was due to adverse childhood experiences, toxic stress, and intergenerational trauma. It was only through the structural changes in my brain, resulting from Davanloo's Intensive Short Term Dynamic Psychotherapy, that I regained my life and experienced hope.

I am also deeply grateful for the work of the late Dr. John Bowlby.

I pay homage to all the researchers and clinicians who tirelessly spend their careers working to better understand how our brains and minds function and to treat and comfort those affected by mental illness. I am inspired by their mission to alleviate human suffering.

I couldn't have written this book without the support of my family.

I am blessed to have a group of incredibly loving people who make up my family.

One of the many gifts of my healing has been my ability to understand that I get to choose who constitutes my family. I thank you all for being a part of my life.

Lastly, and with my deepest love, I mention my husband, Tim, and our daughters, Nina and Simrin.

It would have been impossible to have devoted myself to the arduous task of understanding myself and the true narrative of my life in the way that I did without Tim's constant encouragement and active support. I am humbled by his patience and the steady devotion with which he cared for me during this challenging time, especially when I tried (unsuccessfully, may I add) to heal, write this book, prepare for the sleep boards, work, and parent on the same day. I thank him for his unshakable trust in my abilities, his unwavering love for me and my dreams, and his infinite faith in us.

I will be eternally grateful to have been chosen to be Nina and Simrin's mother. I believe my biggest job as their mother is to live my life in a manner that inspires them to be the best human beings possible. It is my hope that my courage to be honest and open about my struggles will free them to live lives that are authentic and true to who they are, not to the unrealistic expectations of others. It is my deepest wish that their existence will be not only free of suffering but also one of joy. It is my desire and hope to see them live lives of their choice.

My heart is full of gratitude and reverence for the universe. I felt connected to its spirit in a very special way every time I wrote a poem. I have no doubt that the words of *Stripping: My Fight to Find Me* came *through* me, not *to* me.

I share them with you from the place of divine connection we all have with each other.

Introduction

Stripping: My Fight to Find Me will take you into my mind, body, brain, and soul as I journey to reclaim my true self.

It is a unique tale that travels through time, yet it is rooted in its timelessness and is grounded in the collective experience of humanity.

My story, as told through this collection of poems, spans decades of my life but cannot be separated from the history of the generations that came before me.

Through my words you will hear and feel what happens when a child experiences loss and trauma. How is it that the world appeared to be the same scary place to me in adulthood and continued to haunt me? How could I grow up to be so sound, accomplished, and highly successful on the outside yet be so fragmented and unintegrated on the inside?

The process of being able to face the reality of our lives is neither easy nor pain free. But the option of living as a prisoner of my past was unacceptable to me.

So I sought help.

Davanloo's Intensive Short Term Dynamic Psychotherapy techniques and the phenomenon of neuroplasticity brought about structural changes in my brain. An understanding of how trauma affects children and of attachment and interpersonal neurobiology played a critical part in the therapeutic process that brought about my healing. That allowed me to let go of my past and embrace my future and full potential as a human being.

I now share my triumph over darkness so others can feel empowered and inspired to do the same and live the life they were meant to.

My poems give a no-holds-barred account of a grueling and raw battle that is at times tough to read. Yet, you will be compelled to keep turning the pages until you get to the last one. But I not only share my fight but also recognize and celebrate my unconscious that defied my suffering and reached out to be healed and loved.

Stripping: My Fight to Find Me journals the intimate and mysterious relationship between science and spirituality, and it shows how they both make up the sacred in us all. It is a story of the triumph of the human spirit, our deep need for connection, and the infinite power of love to heal.

The author on her first birthday in Lethbridge, Alberta, Canada
Photo: Merriman family album

Yearning

To be loved.

To be loved exclusively,
To be loved above all,
To be loved as the only one.

To be loved for all that is whole in me,
To be loved for all that is broken in me.

To be loved for my beauty,
To be loved for my ugly despair.

To be loved for all that I know,
To be loved for all that I don't know.

To be loved for my ecstasy,
To be loved for my agony.

To be loved for all my strengths,
To be loved for all my fears.

To be loved for my joy,
To be loved for my pain.

To be loved for who I am,
To be loved for who I will become.

To be loved exclusively,
To be loved above all,
To be loved as the only one.

To be loved.

My Isolation

My Isolation is my friend.

My Isolation is my friend.
It's that friend that puts me down
And then laughs
And says,
"Just kidding."

My Isolation is my friend.
It's that friend that dares me to jump off a cliff,
Knowing full well
That there is
An abyss down there.

My Isolation is my friend.
It's that friend that tells me it's my only friend
While
Not allowing anyone else
To know me.

My Isolation is my friend.
It's that friend that tells me the night is dark and stormy
While
The sun shines
Clearly and brightly.

My Isolation is my friend.

Or is it?

Sit with Me

Sit with me awhile.
You may feel a little less lonely.

Sit with me awhile.
You may feel a little less lonely.
You may sigh a little less often.
You may breathe a little bit better.

Sit with me awhile.
You may feel a little less lonely.

Sit with me awhile.
Take a deep look in my eyes.
Take your mind off your old troubles.
Take a risk that may pay off.

Sit with me awhile.
You may feel a little less lonely.

Sit with me awhile.
Allow a glance behind the dark curtain.
Allow a chance to silence your frightened screams.
Allow some time to soften the harsh blows.

Sit with me awhile.
You may feel a little less lonely.

Sit with me awhile.
Share your deepest pain with me.
Share your shattered dreams with me.
Share your unspoken fears with me.

Sit with me awhile.
You may feel a little less lonely.

Sit with me awhile.
Let me share your sadness with you.
Let me carry your load for you.
Let me see your unshed tears.

Sit with me awhile.
You may feel a little less lonely.

Sit with me awhile.
Entrust your journey's weariness to me.
Entrust your heart's yearning to me.
Entrust your soul's longing to me.

Sit with me awhile.
You may feel a little less lonely.

Sit with me awhile.
Be still while your despair deserts you.
Be still while your agony retreats.
Be still while your fury is spent.

Sit with me awhile.
You may feel a little less lonely.

Sit with me awhile.
You just might feel a soft cloud's lightness.
You just might hear a new bird sing.
You just might see the early dawn break.

Sit with me awhile.
You may feel a little less lonely.

Sit with me awhile.
You may feel a little less lonely.

I Hear You

I hear you.
From where I sit,
It may not seem like I do,
But I hear you.

I hear you,
Even though I don't nod my head
When you ask me if I'm all right,
But I hear you.

I hear you.
When you say, "Jump, I'll catch you."
I may not jump,
But I hear you.

I hear you
When you say, "Break free."
I may not trust your words,
But I hear you.

I hear you
When you say I'm strong.
I may not feel that strength,
But I hear you.

I hear you
When you say, "It'll be all right."
I may not believe you,

But I hear you.

I hear you
When I move away
To escape my pain,
But I still hear you.

I hear you
When I wish you would be quiet,
So I am the only one I listen to,
But I still hear you.

I hear you,
Even when I don't want to.
So I can pretend that I'm all alone,
But I still hear you.

I hear you,

So don't stop talking.

Wasteland

The earth is dry and parched.
The sun's been blazing for days.
The tumbleweed is shifting restlessly
In the stagnant, foul air.

The vultures are dying.
The sky is an empty canvas,
No clouds to help make shadows
On the burning desert floor.

Miles of broken glass lay hidden
Under the barren land.
Hollow voices echo back and forth,
Saying nothing much at all.

Trees are mourning
The loss of their leaves,
Bent over to show their grief,
Looking for a drop of water
Foolishly
In vain.

Carcasses lay scattered around
With silent tales of woe:
Untold, unheard, unmourned.

It's a wasteland.

No More

No more
Is my decision.
It comes from the spring
That runs deep inside,
The spring that has always been there,
Flowing steadily and constantly:
At times soundlessly,
At times with the hint of a whisper,
At times clamoring to be heard,
Agitated and restless
With a force that awakens.

No more
Is my choice.
To listen to my heart beating,
To the flow of this spring
In unity and in serene oneness
With the precious tranquility
That lies in its center
In harmony with the truth:
My truth, my essence,
The only truth that matters.

No more
Is my intuition.
No longer denying my experience
Of nestling in the womb of the earth,
Embraced by its cool, moist core;

Sucking on its fragrant and familiar breast
Under the canopy of its comforting quiet
Over many moons and many lifetimes.

No more
Is my resolve.
To know my own truth
Over the empty noises that insist on being heard,
Cloaked in the veils of anonymity
Or bullying and demanding,
Always looking to shatter my image in a million pieces,
Untrue and unrecognizable.

No more
Is my voice.
To invite you in,
To declare my love,
To spread my joy,
To share my fears,
To ask for more,
To sing my song,
To say my truth,
To say good-bye,

To say
No more.

The author on her first day of school in
Coalhurst, Alberta, Canada
Photo: Merriman family album

Shutters

You've done your job well
For the years you've been on guard.

No light has seen the inside
Of this dwelling that I call home.

The carnage, the darkness, the shadows
Would have been a bit too daunting,

The gory details of this bloodbath
Etched and inerasable;

The shame of all my secrets,
Dirty and too heavy to bear.

You've done your job well
For the years you've been on guard.

What a successful reign you've had,
Full of absolute control:

Not a shiny panel out of place,
Not a crack in your pristine veneer,

Shielding me through the storms,
Concealing me from the sun.

Your loyalty, your devotion
For my protection, strong and clear.

You've done your job well
For the years you've been on guard.

The outside paint is cheery,
Butterflies dancing by.

The neighborhood sounds are common,
Comforting and anchoring all the time.

A lawnmower chugalugs in the distance.
A sprinkler sings right outside.

The ice cream truck calls sweetly
With its jingling chimes and rhymes.

You've done your job well
For the years you've been on guard.

But this placid facade is a brilliant hoax.
It's fake, it's false, it's forged.

The tempest that lies behind
Is what's faithful to the truth.

The years of missing sunlight
Have decayed me to my core.

You cover up my rotting, putrid flesh.
You hide my naked glare.

You've done your job well
For the years you've been on guard.

Now I'm begging you on this day,
Be done with this cruel farce.

This is not sweet shelter you give
But a bondage of my heart.

You leave me sad, confused, and mad,
Frightened, and frozen to the bone.

Have mercy on me, please.
Find yourself another home.

You've done your job well
For the years you've been on guard.

Now I dream of shattering this nightmare
To embrace the world outside.

I crave the caress of my demons.
I lust for the ghosts of my past.

My days are dead and barren.
At night I long for someone unknown.

Let me run with the wild, wet wind.
Let me burn in the raging fire.

You've done your job well
For the years you've been on guard.

I don't need your sad protection.
I don't want to be your slave.

I'm in love with my cruel story.
I'm in awe of my ugly scars.

They're mine, they're mine, they're mine
For me to proudly show.

The carnage is my teacher.
The darkness is my guide.

You did your job really well
For the years you were on guard.

Cry

These precious gems are frozen.
They lie hiding in my broken heart.
I wonder,
Is it really beating
Or
Barely keeping me alive?

These precious gems are frozen
In my muddled thoughts somewhere,
Locked up in a distant tower,
Wishing to escape somehow.

These precious gems are frozen
Underneath the polite mask I wear.
My face feels heavy; my smile is forced.
I'm secretly fatigued, and I'm frightened.

These precious gems are frozen
In a private place deep down,
Speaking a language of isolation,
Their words faint and incoherent.

These precious gems are frozen
In the depths of my lonely soul:
Panicked, struggling to find a way out,
Aching to break free once and for all.

These precious gems are frozen,
Mesmerized by the glistening rocks below,
Paralyzed at the edge of the waterfall,
Longing to be smashed into oblivion.

These precious gems are frozen,
Dazzling, bewitching, and gaudy;
Reflecting light like a diamond
Lacking any brilliance of their own:

Pointless,
Useless,
Worthless.

These precious gems are frozen,
Guiltily craving the warmth of light,
Unknowingly coveting its affectionate glow,
Terrified of being swept away
By the force of the flood.

A Glimpse

I look across a crowded room.
No reason.
I see no one I know.
I'm surprised that I'm disappointed.

I rejoin the present:
The good-natured banter,
The back-and-forth of my friends,
The same old jokes and tired stories:
Comfortable, predictable.
I bask in the warmth of my circle.

I feel a tap on my shoulder.
I turn around with a ready smile
To greet a friend
Or say hello to a stranger,

But there's no one there.

I cool my flushed forehead
With the champagne flute in my hand.
The room stands still:
Empty, soundless, airless.

I feel a soft squeeze on my elbow.
I jump,
Startled,
Not wanting to be drawn into nothingness again.

But it's my friend
Looking at me with a silent question in his eyes:
Are you all right?
I smile back,
Reassuring him with an answer.
That's the truth
And a lie
At the same time.

I doubt myself.
It's been a long day.
Wake up.
Shut down this world of make-believe.
Focus on the notes of the music playing.
Listen to the clinks of the ice cubes
As they make their way
Into a smart cocktail.
Savor the tantalizing aromas in the air.
Let the sparkle in this room seduce you.

I hear someone call my name,

But
I'm the only one who does.

A kind look goes around my friends' faces.
She's tired.
Go get her another drink.

Maybe I am exhausted,

Yet
The sound of my name
Stays in the air.

It rings in my ear.
It tingles down my spine.
It pulses in my blood.
It invades my insides.

There is no more denying the lure of this call.
It insists on being heard.

I cover my ears.
It begs,
Listen to me.

I close my eyes.
It pleads,
Look at me.

I hold my breath.
It implores,
Feel me.

I trust myself.
I'm sane.
I'm awake.
I'm alive.
I listen in silence.
I stand absolutely still.
I surrender my soul.

The call is clear:
It comes from an ancient source.
It comes from a familiar place.
It comes from within me.

I understand it.
I know it.
I recognize it.

I search through the portal of my memories.
I ransack the lonely moments I store.
With a pounding heart
I hear your haunted whisper.

I hunger
For a glimpse of you.

As I walk back tonight,
A glorious sorrow washes over me.
Even though it crushes my heart,
I welcome it.
I relish it.
I embrace it.

I'm ready for the joy of the reunion.
There's no mistaking my feverish excitement
In the promised ecstasy
Of rediscovering you.

I hear you.
I feel you.

I remember you.

I ache
For a glimpse of you.

As I make love to the night
With reckless abandon,
I search for your face
In this fearless encounter.

I restlessly writhe.
I shudder, I sigh.
I moan as I burn
With my forlorn desire,

Teased by the moon,
Tortured by the stars,
Finally
Sweet mercy:
A glimpse
In the bliss of release.

I hear you.
I feel you.
I know you.

I see you.

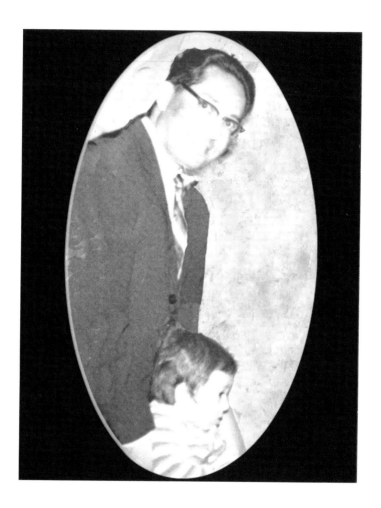

The author and her father, Dr. J. G. S. Merriman,
in Lethbridge, Alberta, Canada
Photo: Merriman family album

I Don't Want to Let You Go

I'm not ready.
It's way too soon.
Please
Let me hide
In your warm embrace.
I feel safe; I feel loved.
I don't want to let you go.

I'm not ready.
It's way too soon.
I haven't yet
Memorized the sound of your voice.
Let me hear you sing one more lullaby.
I feel calm; I feel loved.
I don't want to let you go.

I'm not ready.
It's way too soon.
I still need to remember
The colors of your eyes,
So I may recognize you
Over the uncrossable distance.
I feel seen; I feel loved.
I don't want to let you go.

I'm not ready.
It's way too soon.
I now breathe easy,

Knowing that you lie next to me,
Keeping watch over my gently beating heart.
I feel protected; I feel loved.
I don't want to let you go.

I'm not ready.
It's way too soon.
We just got past the awkward introduction.
You've barely begun
To tell me who you are.
I'm hanging on to your every word.
I feel intrigued; I feel loved.
I don't want to let you go.

I'm not ready.
It's way too soon.
The silence between us
Has just now become our comfortable companion,
Making words unnecessary and unimportant.
I feel understood; I feel loved.
I don't want to let you go.

I'm not ready.
It's way too soon.
I finally see
The light that travels with you
After roaming the dark, lonely streets,
Searching for you, yearning for you.
I feel found; I feel loved.
I don't want to let you go.

I'm not ready.
It's way too soon.
I reverently
Touch your precious face with my eyes shut tight
So I can conjure you up whenever I desire.
I feel powerful; I feel loved.
I don't want to let you go.

I'm not ready.
It's way too soon.
I just discovered
The simple, sweet pleasure of seeing you again
After suffering the indecent pain of our separation.
I feel relief; I feel loved.
I don't want to let you go.

I'm not ready.
It's way too soon.
We have so much
More to share.
There are a million things to still talk about.
I feel energized; I feel loved.
I don't want to let you go.

I'm not ready.
It's way too soon
For me to even dare
Ask you why you left
So suddenly, so quietly, so cruelly.
No kiss good-bye. No "I'll see you again."
I feel unsettled. I feel confused.

I don't want to let you go.

I'm not ready.
It's way too soon.
I don't want to make this easy for you.
I demand an explanation. I want an apology,
But deep down
I just want you
To stay with me forever.
I feel desperate. I feel frantic.
I don't want to let you go.

I'm not ready.
It's way too soon.
How will I feel hope
Come shining through as the sun rises
Without you
Describing its beauty and promise?
How can I trust
It will come back to me
After retiring
Into the serenity of the night?
I feel terror. I feel despair.
I don't want to let you go.

I'm not ready.
It's way too soon.
I don't want to let you go.

Stripping

It's not enough.

Don't say that again.

I'm falling apart,
Looking to flee.
I'm spent.

The first to go was the smile.

I took it off the day you didn't smile back.
I was unaware of its fake charm,
Its hollow promise of glee.
I was taken in by its unnatural brightness
Over many years of acquaintanceship,
Too close to see its game.

It was hard to let it go.
I felt naked
And unprotected,
Awkwardly
Looking for something else
To cover up my unease.

Would a witty story do
Instead of a jolly smile?
I have plenty of tales to tell,

Many a story to share.

The world applauds Scheherazade
For her creativity,
Her imagination, and
Her guile;
Seducing Shahyar with a new story
Night after night,
Her words weaving a magic web
Of suspense, intrigue, and desire.
But she had nothing on me, for
Her storytelling went on for
Just a thousand and one nights.

Mine
Has spanned
A lifetime.

My tales are true and thoughtful,
Well told, riveting, and captivating.
They will engage you.
They will entertain you.
They will enchant you.
You will hunger to hear more.
The time will fly by.
I will amuse you.
I will fascinate you.
I will mesmerize you.

I always have.

I noticed something amiss
When you didn't nod.
You didn't blink.
You didn't move.
You didn't say, "What happened next?"

I spoke faster.
I spoke louder,
Trying to silence the voices in my head,
Desperate to hide my despair.

The silence from you was deafening,
So the stories were the next to go.

It was hard to let them go.
I felt naked
And unprotected,
Stubbornly
Looking for something else
To cover up my distress.

The perpetual persuasion
To disrobe and reveal
Is wearing me down,
To do as I'm told.

But I've still got some fight
Stuck deep in my soul,
Many more side streets
To discover and explore.

Wandering, fanciful, unguided,
Like a vagabond carelessly drifting
Toward an unknown horizon,
I'm deliriously dizzy
As I spin around in circles:
Elated, ecstatic, euphoric.

The rush is now over.
My cold reality is setting in.
I'm back,
Standing still
Right where I started.

It didn't work.

I still hear your incessant call to undress,
Like the ceaseless roar of battle.
I'm consumed.
I'm bone weary.
I'm incapable of simple thought.

With a weak whimper
The map to nowhere
Was the next to go.

It was hard to let it go.
I felt naked
And unprotected,
Frantically
Looking for something else
To cover up my torment:

No smiles as our greeting,
No stories as our bridge,
No flights to neverland.
What's left for me to show you?
What remains for me to say?

I'm battered, I'm bruised.
I'm depleted.
I'm confused.

I give up.

It's time to go home.

Home
Is a place I know,
My secret hideaway.

No one else has the key to this crypt.
It's quiet, it's secluded, it's dark.
It beckons me in my sleep.
It calls to me when I'm awake,
Like an ancient snake charmer,
Hypnotizing me
When I'm in too deep.

I'm back.
What a relief.

I greedily inhale the comfort of the familiar, damp, musty walls.
As I lower myself down on to the cool stone floor,

I close my weary eyes.

I finally don't hear your constant refrain.

Peace at last.
I'm home.

But I still feel naked
And unprotected,
Hysterically
Looking for anything
To cover up my wretched pain.

I have searched for serenity
In the troubled silence that surrounds me.
I have prayed for relief
In my godless abode with no faith.
I have sought guidance
From the anxious voices of my mind.
I have journeyed toward a destination
In a never-ending maze.
I have demanded the truth
While living a lie.

I'm falling apart.
Looking to flee,
I'm spent.

I'm paralyzed, I'm numb.
I'm at the brink of oblivion,
Yet

I still hear your voice in this emptiness.

I surrender.

I strip with great care,
Slowly peeling off each precious layer
Bravely, delicately, completely.

I'm surprised at my gentleness as I uncover my festering wounds.
I'm overwhelmed with tenderness as I embrace my buried anguish.
I weep at the sight of my forbidden pain.
I lovingly tend to my ravaged heart,
Soothing its piercing cries of silent suffering.
I am taken aback at the violence of the gushing geyser of my grief.
It knocks me off my feet.
I falter, and I fumble.
I feel my scars still throbbing after all these years.
I remember being stabbed
Again and again by my unseen loneliness.

I'm grotesque, I'm disfigured.
I'm deeply ashamed.
It's all been revealed.
No secrets remain.

In this nothing
Do I find everything?

Is it enough?

Forbidden Love

Just thinking of loving you
Seems so felonious
As I steal a quick glance
From the corner of my eye
Cautiously, quietly,
Not wanting to be found,
Looking at you,
Hungering for you,
Wishing
To be one with you.

I take my sweet time
As I breathlessly embrace you,
Greedy to touch you,
Feel you,
Consume you,

All from a distance
That shields me,
Shelters me.
My safety
Lies in my concealment,
My comfort
A gift of my invisibility.

A wildfire burns madly through me,
Yet I'm unscorched
And untouched.

It's my guilty pleasure
To gaze upon you
As you adorn yourself
Unabashedly,
Unhurriedly,
Oh, so lovingly
Unaware of my presence.

I am lost
In the mysterious invitation
Of your smile.
I am mesmerized
By your resplendent beauty.
I am tipsy
With a drunken happiness
As I catch the reflection
From your flushed face.
You have bewitched me
With a wordless spell.

I float on a cloud of exuberant ecstasy.
I'm infused with your sublime perfection.

You're lit, you're aglow.
I am powerless to resist you.

I tremble with trepidation
As I reach out to touch you,
Desperate to be discovered,
Dying to be recognized.

I stop in my tracks,
The distance between you and me
Suddenly uncrossable.

I am powerless to advance.

My heart is racing.
My palms are sweating.
I am terror stricken
At my unforgivable lapse
Into the insanity
Of daring to dream,
Of deserving your delight.

I am sickened
By the angry roughness of my scabs
As I yearn to worship
The sensuous curves of your body.
I see my plainness
In the reflection of your radiance.
I notice the sad dullness
Of all that I see
As I am tempted
To lose myself in your deep, dark eyes.

The heaviness in my heart annoys me
As I covet a taste of your effervescence.

I have nothing important to say
As I carefully listen
To your fascinating words.

Your radiance brings me no joy
As I stare at my pallid complexion.

I'm disheartened.
I'm discouraged.
I'm repulsed by my need.
I mercilessly flog myself
For wanting this love.

This fantasy of pleasure
Has rocked me to my core.

I'm restless.
I'm enraged.
I'm furious with myself
For repenting unwillingly,
For wanting this bliss.

My impotence disgusts me.
My misgivings are repulsive.
My caution is revolting.
My inhibition no longer serves me.

I am not ugly.

It's the mirror
That is broken.

Your glory is mine.
My shame is yours.
Your virtue is mine.

My guilt is yours.
Your loftiness is mine.
My despondency is yours:

Shared,
Fused,
Divine,
Sanctioned.

I'll Say Good-Bye if You Stay Forever

It must be done.
I know that in my heart,
But I can't say the word.
I just can't walk away.

Let's make a few deals.
Let's discuss this a bit.
Let's see how this sad end
Could be a hopeful beginning.

Will You

Will you
Come to me in my dreams
On the dark, stormy nights
Of tossing and turning,
Of trying to shut out
The sound
Of the howling wind outside?

It will comfort me if you did.
It will calm my panicked soul.
It will soothe my many fears.
It will help me
Drift into an easy sleep.

The soft sound of your breathing
Is the only lullaby I need
To take me safely
Into the promise
Of a calm and peaceful morning.

Will you
Show me what you see
When you look at me?
It will help me
On the days
When fog clouds my mirror.

I often feel lost,
Unable to feel,
Hopelessly bereft of my limbs,
Stripped of my will to move
In the direction of the light.

On those days
I hover
Between a dead, silent numbness
And a harrowing pain
That leaves me keening,
Tortured by the terror
Of no longer
Being able to tell them apart.

In those moments
I am powerlessly led
By my blurred thoughts,
Unable to see clearly,
Unbelieving of what I see.

Will you?

It's Okay

You can let it all out.
I know what it's all about.

I can see your crazed eyes,
Even when you turn away.

I can feel your crushing pain
Right through your brave, little smile.

I am singed by your burning flames
From a billion miles away.

You can let it all out.
I know what it's all about.

Take a step closer to me.
I promise I won't step back.

Look me in the eye.
I promise I won't look away.

Show me your savage beast.
I promise I won't be scared.

You can let it all out.
I know what it's all about.

You can rest assured that I see
The beauty in your ugly scars.

You can trust me to be tender
With the demons that you hide.

You can let your guard down
And visit me with your lawless fury.

You can let it all out.
I know what it's all about.

You have it all together, but
You're allowed to say, "I am not fine."

You walk tall and proud, but
You're entitled to feel broken.

You tell your story with poise and grace, but
You're permitted to wildly cry out in pain.

You can let it all out.
I know what it's all about.

Stop hitting yourself with this furious frenzy.
I am here to take the blows.

Give me all your silent screams.
I will give them a voice.

Don't worry about my pain.
I can catch you with my broken arms.

You can let it all out.

It's okay.

I have known
What it's all about.

Sunset at a lake in Jim Thorpe, Pennsylvania, USA
Photo: Timothy J. Carlsen

Let Me

The sunlight lingers awhile,
Reluctant to say good-bye,
Still generous,
Still warm,
Unhurried in its exit,
Languorously
Stretching over the lake:
Rapturous,
Blissful,
Satiated.

It's been a good day.

The sounds
Of the approaching evening
Make it lazily smile:
Porch doors
Swinging open and shut,
Bicycles
Being strewn carelessly
Across front lawns,
A few straggling rowboats
Being hustled ashore
Before darkness dances on the lake,
Gentle waves
Playfully flirting with the oars
As they break the quiet
Over the glistening water.

It's been a good day.

Let me welcome you to my world.
Come sit by me.
While I say good-bye to the sun,
Watch me
As I prepare
To say hello
To the stars and the moon.
I am so happy to share the magic of the sundown with you.

Let me show you the fireworks in the sky.
Come sit by me.
Look
At the colors that came
To see off the glorious sun:
Oranges, reds, yellows, pinks,
And holy crimson;

All lining up in the clear, blue sky
Reverently,
Following the sun
As it descends into the lake.
I am so grateful
To share the quiet beauty of this twilight with you.

Let me take you into the house with me.
Come sit by me.
Tell me how you've been.
I've missed you terribly.
You look tired

And sad.
I hope you weren't worrying about me.

Let me wipe your tears away.
Come sit by me.
Lay your head on my shoulder.
Close your eyes
So I may softly kiss your pain away.
Feel my love for you
In the gentleness of my touch
As I caress your weary face.
Allow your sorrow to leave you
Like the sun just did
With grace,
With celebration,
With certitude.

Let me light the candles around us
Slowly,
One by one.
Come sit by me.
Watch with me in wonderment
As their radiant glow
Dresses the dusk that surrounds us,
The darkness
No longer
Unknown
And unfamiliar
But a longtime friend:
Tranquil,
At peace,

Luminous,
Swathing our leaking souls,
Mending,
Plugging,
Filling us
With a calm stillness
And an exciting promise.

Let me pull you into the ebullience of the evening.
Come sit by me
As the hushed dusk
Makes way
For the jaunty assurance of the night,
Of a festive family feast.
My heart beats faster
As I hear the showers turn on.
I feel the warm water
Joyously cascade down my body,
Washing off
The playful sand from the day,
Carefully preserving
The sweet kisses of the sun;
Cleansing me,
Loving me,
Rejuvenating me.

I feel alive.

It's been a good day.

Let me share my world with you.

Stay seated by me.
Luxuriate with me.
In the voices that surround us,
Behold the familiar faces of those who join us.
Help me spin a timeless cocoon around our world.

Let me love you.
Let me cherish you.
Let me keep you.

Arousal

My slumber went unnoticed:
No reason for detection,
No cause for concern,
No need to wake up from this deep sleep.

I opened the door
To a gentle tremor
Innocently,
Unsuspecting
Of this avalanche that I was hiding.

Crazy, Hungry Love

You're good.
You're damn good.
I'll give you that.

I thought you knew me
Better than I knew myself,
So
I let you paint my portrait
In all the strokes and colors
You chose,
Only
To have a lost woman
Stare wildly back at me.

I didn't know any better.
I was hungry for love.
I was lonesome,
So
You had me believing
That
I was the crazy one.

I laughed at your jokes
On all the cruel punch lines,
Thinking you were funny
Despite my buried unease
At their sadistic twists and turns.

I didn't know any better.
I was hungry for love.
I was lonesome,
So
You had me believing
That
I was the crazy one.

I slept in broad daylight
When you deemed it was night,
Roughly pulling down the blinds,
Convincing myself it was dark
By forcing my eyes shut.

I didn't know any better.
I was hungry for love.
I was lonesome,
So
You had me believing
That
I was the crazy one.

I swear I heard the voices
That you said tormented you,
Taunted you, and scared you,
Even though we were engulfed
By a sullen silence
As we sat in an insulated isolation.

I didn't know any better.
I was hungry for love.

I was lonesome.
So
You had me believing
That
I was the crazy one.

I was happy to give you all that I had
With my love and simple devotion,
Content to be running on empty,
Only to be accused to have
Mercilessly starved you.

I didn't know any better.
I was hungry for love.
I was lonesome,
So
You had me believing
That
I was the crazy one.

I trusted you every time
You said it was love
That you embraced me with,
Even though it felt like
Being wrapped tight with barbed wire,
The shooting pains
Rendering me breathless and dizzy.

I didn't know any better.
I was hungry for love.
I was lonesome,

So
You had me believing
That
I was the crazy one.

I hated all those that you said
Had wronged you,
Doubted your brilliance,
Scoffed at your captivating charm,
Never noticing the glassy dullness
Of your clouded eyes.

Sadly
I didn't know any better.
I was hungry for love.
I was lonesome,

So
I believed
That
I was the crazy one.

Cold

I'm falling
Straight out of the sky.

Am I spinning slowly
Or
Am I perishing
In the blink of an eye?

I would have made it home
Had I been abseiling
Down this vortex
With my safety rope.

I tugged softly,
Trusting you would be there
Right where you were supposed to be,
Ready to break my fall.

But I kept on plummeting.

In those milliseconds,
There were
No flashbacks of my life's highlights,
No parading visions of my loved ones,
No consortium of my life's regrets,

Just
Me
Feeling

Cold.

Entreaty

I catch a flicker
From under the ice.

Is that you?

Down here at the bottom,
It's bitterly cold.

The water is sluggish.
It's murky and gray.

It bites at my flesh.
I'm taken aback by the pain.

I burn in this frost
As it pierces my hide.

I wonder in this vacuum,
Am I dead or alive?

I hear a murmur
From under the ice.

Is that you?

Down here at the bottom,
It's eerily quiet.

The rare sounds that do visit
Are muffled and weak.

I strain to detect them
As I force myself to stay still.

This silence is not tranquil.
It's harsh, and it's loud.

My desolation is screaming
With a soundless despair.

I catch a movement
From under the ice.

Is that you?

Down here at the bottom,
It's puzzling; it's unclear.

I make out an auger,
Bore a hole through the ice.

A blush of timid hope
Teases my motionless heart.

A tunnel of light
Slips through the crack in the shield,

A way out perhaps.
Could this be freedom at last?

I catch a flash of color
From under the ice.

Is that you?

Down here at the bottom,
There's excitement in the air.

The splendor of the jig
Brings us all out of hiding.

Hungry perch greedily gawk.
Reclusive bass feign indifference,

The seductive dance of the lure
Reassuringly familiar and uncomfortably unknown.

I've been desperate to be found.
I've been waiting to be caught.

I feel such longing
From under the ice.

Is that you?

Down here at the bottom,
I'm utterly alone.

I spy shoals of hypnotic fish
Swimming gracefully as one.

Their synchronicity, their togetherness
Unmask my isolation.

I hunger for their friendship
As I shyly move away.

I cry out for their protection
As I stoically pretend to be brave.

I secretly ache to belong
As I sit proudly by myself.

I'm desperate to escape
From under the ice.

Is that you?

Down here at the bottom,
I'm swiftly suffocating.

I'm begging you to give me a sign
That you know that I even exist.

Once again lower the jig
Or just spear me to bits.

I wish I could feel.
I wish I could move.

But I'm hopelessly stuck
In this torpid existence.

Please,
Please,
Please

Tell me.

Is that you?

Unnoticed

I turn away
Every time
You look at me.

It's not personal.

It's just that
I don't want to think right now.
Come to think about it,
I don't want to feel right now either.

I'm tired.
This load is hard to carry.
It wears me down.

I need to rest now.
I need to shut off this pain.

I've been busy in my head.
I didn't notice you.
Did I turn away again?

As I said,
It's not personal.

I need to solve some problems.
I must come up with some smart answers.
I have to find a way out

Of this maze
Of chaos and confusion.

I'm lightheaded
As I keep hitting the same wall
And keep going back
To the same bolted door,
Hoping to exit from this nightmare.

Oh,
You're still here.
I'm surprised.
I told you I didn't mean to turn away.
You know it's not personal.

It's just that I'm crushed
By the weight of my worries.
There's no way for me
To invite you in right now.
It's not the right time,
Nor the right place.

I promise
It's truly not personal.
Please go away.
You're making me nervous
By sticking around.

I'm used to myself
Being my constant companion.
These fears are familiar.

This alarming darkness
Is an old friend,
Its terror well known,
Its seclusion quite comfortable.

Why are you still here?
Please go away.

Are you listening?

Remember,
It's not personal.

You're pushing me to panic.
I don't want you to see me.

I
Will
Now
Turn
Away.

Just know
It's not personal.

Lanced

I stand still
In this cascade,

Feeling every tingle
Of its splashdown.

I hear every cheer
Of these rapids,

My skin splitting open
With an exquisite, raw pleasure.

I feel alive,

Only to discover

That
In this oneness,
I am

Alone.

Hunger

No matter how full I am,
I remain
Incessantly hungry.

I can devour you for days
And still
Be famished.

This emptiness has pushed me
Into a life
Of endless wandering.

I'm crazy,
Waving frantically
Right here
In front of your face.
Do you know me?

When you hold me in your arms,
Nothing exists
But us
In this closeness.
Do you feel me?

I'm screaming out in pain
As loud
As I possibly can,
Telling you that I'm starving.

Do you hear me?

I've stripped down
To absolute nothing,
Standing here naked,
Scared, and exposed.
Do you see me?

I ache to know.
Am I yours?

The beach, Jumby Bay Island, Antigua
Photo: Timothy J. Carlsen

Allure

It's a bright, sunny morning.
The rustle of the tropical breeze
Awakens my senses,
Its flirtatious whispers
Electrifying
My sun-drenched body.

I lift my face to the sky
In worship of the day,
A deep peace
Bathing my heart.

The amorphous white billows above,
Intentional
Yet drifting,
Purposeful
Yet mysterious,
Curious.
I wonder
Who anxiously awaits them
In distant lands.
Who do they long to reunite with
After their passage?

I close my eyes,
Compelled to rejoice
In this perfect moment,
The warmth of the blazing sun

Suffusing my heart
With joy.

I pay homage to life.

The gentle sounds of the waves
Lapping the sandy beach
In a rhythmic game of hide-and-seek
Silently and suddenly
Ambush me
Into a hypnotic trance.

One moment
The water
Daring to come up
And seek my buried toes,
Caressing them
With its loving coolness;
In the next,
Cruelly deserting them,
Leaving them
Bereft, baffled, and lonely.

I lift my face to the horizon,
Catching the harsh glare
Spread over the crystal bay.

A sadness with no boundaries
Strikes my heart.

I plead with the callous waves
To ignore the lure of the sea.

Oh, please, can you stay?
Or just let me walk away.

Recoil

I beg of you,
Stop looking at me like this:

The wordless comfort,
The unspoken understanding.
The quiet love in your eyes

Is
Unraveling
Me.

Could you please
Stop talking to me like this?

Your gentle tone,
Your encouraging words,
This praise you give

Are
Confusing
Me.

I implore of you.
End your patient standoff with me:

Its comforting thrum,
Its constant existence,
Its breathtaking vastness

Are
Terrifying
Me.

Could you please
Change your tone with me?

No demands,
No reproach,
No reprove.

This
Is
Unbearable
For
Me.

I
Recoil.

Agony

I don't want you to leave,
But I can't bear it when you stay.

Help Me

It was scarcely a whisper
That escaped the long hush,

A plea undiscovered
In a language unknown.

It was missed all along
By the lightkeeper on call,

Eclipsed by the storm,
Oppressed by the calm,

Some part of a delusion

Or a chimera
Perhaps.

The author, age six, in Lethbridge, Alberta, Canada
Photo: Merriman family album

Lost and Found

The harsh lights
Abruptly
Flood the warehouse,
Rudely
Waking us
From our fitful sleep.
There's no time
To primp and polish,
No chance
To clear our thoughts.

We stumble
To the display room,
Pushing and shoving
To get in front,
For we all want the spots
That face the door
So the limelight
Can shine on us
In the hope
That we are seen.

Fresh promise
Cautiously
Raises its head,
Hesitant
To boldly show up
After the letdown

Of the days before,
Mindful
Of the disquiet in the air,
Flinching at the panic in our eyes.

The morning goes by briskly.
Many of my friends,
Some new,
Some old,
Go home,
Claimed by their special buds
Among squeals of joy
And cries of relief,
All of them
Smothered with tender hugs and sweet kisses.

I'm trying
Really, really hard
To keep the smile on my face
From uncontrollably quivering.
Every moment that passes
Is an impossible endeavor
To hold back my terrified tears.
It's now taking everything in me
Not to tremble and shiver
And keep on hiding my fears.

I'll be good,
I promise.
I'll be quiet,
You'll see.

I'll fuss no more
That I pledge for sure.
Do you want me to enter
Into a covenant with you?
I'll sign on the dotted line
To every one of your demands.

I must have done harm.
I'm sure I've been wrong.
I don't understand
All my follies.
I can't comprehend
Most of my mistakes,
But please forgive me.
I'm so sorry.
Please come and get me.
I'm so scared.

I need to be found
So
I'm not lost here
Forever.

Confetti

It's like
Happy colors
Exploded in the sky,

A sense of enchantment,
A feeling of no worries.

These tiny dollops
Of sweet rapture
Lightheartedly sashay.

This celestial parade seen
From the meadow down below—
It's picture perfect, it's pristine, and it's poised.

But the longer I scan
And the closer I look,
The more I don't see.

My eyes don't want to move
From this spurious celebration,
Stubbornly embracing the sham.

I defiantly still wear
The emperor's new clothes,
Clinging desperately to my charade.

It's getting damp and very cold.
I'm stiff, and I'm sore
As I gaze up to the dark sky:

Not a kaleidoscope in sight,
Not a stitch of make-believe garb.

I'm stripped of my illusions.
I'm depleted,
And I'm bare.

I've no place to look but up,
The firmament proudly luminous
Despite its rift with the stars.

It's like
Pieces of my mind
Exploded in the sky:

A sense of veracity,
A feeling of truthfulness,

The sad smithereens
Of my suffering
Silently floating in the air.

This hellish spectacle is seen
From the coffin in the ground.
It's relentless, it's raw, but it's real.

The longer I observe,
The closer I examine,
The more I comprehend.

The gray ashes are still in place.
The plumes of dirty smoke in no denial.
My fragments are in no mood of withdrawal.

I say hello to my damaged heart.
I greet my long-lost lonely minds.
I discover my cruel, continuous confinement.

My eyes are burning.
My mouth is dry.
My voice falters.

Yet
I'm relieved
That
My truth still exists.

Masterpiece

This room is floating.

I see no floor.
I sense no windows.
I feel no walls.

Is it a circle?
Is it a square?

I can't tell,

And

I really don't care anymore.

Everywhere I look,
I see the savage splatter
Of my past,
The wild orgy of this painting
Embedded in my mind's sight,
Staring at me from all directions,

Every single drip of paint
No longer content
To just quietly
Find a place
In the background
Of my unprimed canvas;

Every frantic stroke
No longer willing
To be part of the wicked web
That cruelly concealed
The endless nights of terror
That viciously veiled
The sepulchral scenes of starvation
That noisily drowned out
The tales of tortured loneliness.

As I wield the handle of my brush,
I drip paint with a wild frenzy.
I slash the demons
That have tormented me.
I stomp on the ghosts
That have abandoned me.
I break free of the chains
That have imprisoned me.

Spent,
Still
Serene,

I slowly step back.

I am finally able to see
My very own Pollack.

It
Is
Red.

My Red Sea

An unmemorable injury,
An unremarkable wound.

It's all healed up now,
Barely a blemish to be seen.

But there's a persistent little itch
That just won't go away.

And a pesky, dull ache
That plagues me on some days.

Since this happened so long ago,
It's a phantom, I have no doubt.

I turn over to scratch
The slight scar that I can feel.

It's bumpy, and it's rough.
It's a bit raised and on my back.

A soft touch, a little attention.
That's probably all that it really needs.

I'm sure it's nothing more
Than a to-be-expected slight unease.

I'm gentle, and I'm careful
As I rub on my past hurt.

But it's as if I unknowingly carry
The ancient staff that Moses did.

My skin angrily parts
At the edges of my old scar.

I'm now searching for my dry ground
In a violent stream of warm, wet venom.

My decay delights in its discharge,
My tiny wound now a gaping hole.

Its flow is relentless and unabating.
It's rotten, and it's rancid.

The more I plug this crevasse,
The wider it splits itself open.

The drama of this putrefaction
Stubbornly refuses to run its course.

I'm in a never-ending nightmare,
Whether I'm asleep or I'm awake.

This poison leaves me incoherent,
Perpetually rotting and defacing.

I'm in ceaseless and painful suffering
With no crossing yet in sight,

All from an unmemorable injury,
All from an unremarkable wound.

Addicted

I walk on sand.
My sand shifts with the wind.
It runs after the outlying horizon,
Carelessly leaving me groundless.

I walk on sand,
Loyal to its invariable whimsies,
Longing for its fickle love,
Accepting of its infinite, illicit transgressions.

I walk on sand
Even as it brutally blinds me,
Blasting my bare, trusting face
When propelled by a cruel, stormy gale.

I walk on sand,
Crippled by my craving of its wayward flights,
Shackled by the bottomless pit that it conceals,
Imprisoned by my fear of solid ground.

Sanctuary

There's no need
For me to bow my head.
There's no demand
For me to be quiet,
No shoes to be removed.
No shoulders to be covered.

I can come in as I am.

There's no need
For me to hide my despair.
There's no demand
For me to conceal my outrage.
I can wail if I want.
I can whimper if I choose.

I can come in as I am.

There's no need
For me to light a candle.
There's no demand
For me to burn any incense.
I can set my suffering on fire.
I can torch my pain to show

I can come in as I am.

There's no need
For me to fake reverence.
There's no demand
For me to chant empty words.
I can say what I want.
I can feel what I feel.

I can come in as I am.

There's no need
For me to hide my victories.
There's no demand
For me to subdue my allure,
No brilliance to be put down,
No joyful exultation to be squashed.

I can come in as I am.

There's no need
For the storm to die out.
There's no demand
For the tsunami to pass.
I can feel the peace inside.
I can hold on to the safety within.

I can come in as I am.

Surrender

There will be no retreat,
Even though the battle is lost.

I ignore the call
To lay down my weapons.

I continue to fight
Long after the cease-fire,

Stubbornly advancing
Blindly and unprotected,

Bloodied and battered,
Foolishly and falsely bold,

Incognizant of your might,
Unsuspecting of my sorry plight,

Covertly
Longing
To be captured,

Hoping
For
No mercy.

Beim Schlafengehen

My lips are blue
As a cloudless sky
On a cold, blustery day,
Its cheery brightness
Openly deceitful,
Treacherously
Misleading me
To trust
In its frigid warmth.

I spy
Forlorn leaves,
Shriveled,
Rustling in the mournful wind,
Lip-synching to a song
That never was
In the galaxy
Of dead silence.

I hold my breath
And wait
Anxiously
For my pain
To invade me,
Inviting it to suffuse
My insensible self
With its searing sensation,
Beseeching it to conquer me.

I'm not represented
By this noiseless zone
That officiously surrounds me,
For if you could hear
The voices in my head,
You would run
To escape the savagery
With which
They hack me to pieces.

It was beguiling in the beginning,
Being bewitched
By your brooding gaze.
This isolation had me spellbound.
Being cordoned off
Was a relief
Until I learned
That I was not allowed out
From this solitary confinement.

It's April third somewhere.

River Ouse calls again,
Proclaiming its love for me,
Promising me
Protection within its banks
And safety in its channel,
Dangling redemption from its bed.

Who's afraid of Virginia Woolf?
Not I.

I slide down the bank,
Numbness and silence
My faithful companions,
Right by my side
As I'm swiftly accosted
By a cold and tempestuous current.

In this storm
I hear the music.

The somber call of the cellos
Heralds a baleful night.

I stand my ground,
Insistent on finding relief,
Secure in the knowledge
That the rocks in my pocket
Will not let me down.

My fingers work blindly in the dark,
Obsessively
Stroking the sharp, hard edges
Again and again
With a feverish,
Blasphemous excitement.

I'm fixated on the promise
In their immensity

The violins answer my unconscious plea
And gently commence

To burn the fog that encompasses me
Painstakingly
Inch by inch

Until
She
Pierces
The air
With her lament to the stormy skies,

Her voice
Carrying over to the next world,
Powerful and clear,
With its scorn for this story,
Her dolorous melody
For all to hear.

How could you?

Do you see what you've done to her?

No breath,
No blood,
No life.

How could you?

Look at this treacherous water,
Daringly making love to her:
Defiant.
Brazen,

Unrelenting in its assault,
Its illicit intentions and designs
Shamelessly transparent.

How could you?

I demand of you,
Look at her who does not exist,
This empty vessel:
Icy,
Impassive,
Isolated;
Taking small stiff steps
To hide from no one around her,
To escape from everyone inside her.

How could you?

The French horn replies
But with no answers,

Instead bringing violins and witnesses
To the morgue
In the water
Housing the aftermath
Of the cold-blooded massacre.

The river's turbulent flow
Haltingly eases,
Finally
Coming to a stop.

The water is now still
And silent
As the sirens
Circle around me
And
Start
To
Weep,

Their tears
Falling on my stiff face
And my frozen heart.

Not a sound is heard in the forest.
Not a bird is seen in the sky;

Just me and my grief
Cradled in their arms
As they wash away
My ineradicable pain:

Tenderly,
Gently,
Slowly

Stripping
Me of my tattered coverings
That were hiding
The millions of layers of hurt,
Carefully
Dressing the wounds of my broken body,

Touching
The invisible stains on my soul,
Lovingly
Coaxing my loneliness to leave
As they
Caress
My tired spirit.

Is this rain that I feel on my face?
Or the precious gems that I had buried?

I taste my tears.

I weep with the sky,
Showered with the lavender lovings of the clouds
In my bath of milk and honey,
Watching
My shame and sorrow
Drain away.

Her voice
Is
Now
My
Voice.

I proclaim,
I am awake now.
I am clean now.
I am alive now.

I am propelled out of the water,
Unshackled,
Shooting straight into the sky,
Bright, Hot, Radiant, Aglow,
Burning the sun into submission.

Looking down from above,
I see an exodus
Headed toward the banks
Of my holy river.

I need to go home.

Solid ground under my feet,
Not water, not sand.
I stand firm
As I welcome
My lost friends,
My missing breaths,
My stolen laughter,
My robbed smiles,
My unshared kisses,
My unsung songs,
My unmade mistakes,
My untaken journeys,
My uncelebrated successes,
My unheard laments,
My unreceived affections,
My unsaid "I love yous,"
My unworshiped divinity,
My unexpressed adoration,

My untold stories,
My undiscovered glory,
My unfelt anger,
My unseen pain,
My unexperienced fury,
My unnoticed longings,
My uncared-for hunger,
My unacknowledged presence,

My unallowed hope.

They all move toward me,
Cloaked in darkness
Out of the wilderness,
Of the hidden forest:

Haggard,
Drawn,
Exhausted,
Depleted.

One by one,
Hundreds,
Then thousands
Until I lose count
And stop tracking time.

I open my arms
And receive every one of them.

They pierce me.

They enter me.
They fill me.
They are one with me.

They are me:

No longer lost,
No longer scared,
No longer hiding,
No longer wandering.

I am home.

As I fall asleep
On the cool, moist ground of Ouse's bank,
I feel the soft clouds' lightness.
I hear a new bird sing.
I see the early dawn break.

I Wrote These Poems for Myself

I read them when I need to find solace and comfort.
I read them when I need to find the strength to go on.
I read them when I need to be inspired.
I read them when I need to be reminded that I am much bigger
than the fight that I have had to fight.
I read them so I always remember how brave I am.

These poems are my story.

My story is your story

Because I am you.

I Want the Sky

I never knew you existed
From the confines of my captivity,

Blindfolded by the darkness that imprisoned me.
It was impossible
To see
That you were right there,

Enslaved by Erebus since inception.
It was unthinkable for me
To believe
That you were real.

Forever slaying demons and delusions,
It was too exhausting for me
To look up
And notice you.

Even after I was finally free
Somehow, I chose
To ignore
Your all-encompassing presence.

It was safer for me
To deny your existence than
To risk
Your desertion and disappearance.

It took everything in me
To make myself impregnable
And look
For the briefest of moments at you.

It's no longer possible
For me to dismiss my compulsion
To crave
The heady reality of your presence.

I'm in a never-ending battle,
Fighting myself day and night
To not need
The safety of your embrace.

I stomp my feet in outrage at your fickle nature
Rather than admit
I fear
The pleasure of your protection.

Now that I know you exist,
Why can't I just say
I want the sky?

A door in Rajasthan, India
Photo: Sunita Merriman

Permission

To love myself,
I must know who I am.

To know who I am,
I must go back in time.

To find my own voice,
I must silence what you said.

To find my own truth,
I must leave the lies behind.

To live in my light,
I must give myself permission
To make peace with the darkness.

My Stalker

I changed
The locks
On my door.
I scrubbed
The dirty floor.
I white-washed
The bloody walls.
I waved
The smoke of sage
Into
All the hidden corners
And
Every shadow space
I could see.

Then
I lay down with my new lover,

Unenclosed
In
Broad daylight
With my eyes
Wide open
And
My heart
Unlocked,
Taking in
The warmth

Of the smiling sun,
Wrapped tightly
In the promise
Of
A new beginning.

I allowed
The playful waves
Of the ocean
To seduce me

As they
Rushed
Toward me
And immersed me
In their immensity.
I was struck
With a sudden terror
As
I felt you.

I couldn't see you.
I couldn't hear you,

But
I knew
You
Were
Inside
Me.

I had believed
You were a million miles away,

Banished
From my life,
Expelled
From my thoughts,
A horror story
From
My calamitous past.

But you violently
Flung the locked door
Wide open,
The floor
Now
Flooded and cold,
The hidden corners
And the saged shadow spaces
Screaming in my face;

The white walls
Brutally ambushed,
And
The light
Heartlessly eclipsed
By
Your
Darkness.

Soar

I'm still on fire.
Let me freely burn.

Don't hover over me
With your bucket of water.

It won't be enough.
It won't help me much.

I'm still in agony.
Let me feel all my pain.

Don't wrap me up
In your scanty rags.

They won't be enough.
They won't help me much.

You've only seen the tinder burn.
Let me get down to the blue blaze.

I don't want a single log
To escape this inferno.

Just stand back
And watch me brightly burn in my skin.

Stay close to me

But let me writhe in my suffering.

I want this bonfire of my lamentations
To light up the starless sky.

This conflagration will spread
Faster than you think.

It will burn
Through my soul
Soon enough.

Stay with me.

But let me rise from my ashes
On my own.

The author and her daughter Nina in Edison, New Jersey, USA
Photo: Carlsen family album

Le Pardon

You can stop opening the door
And making the introductions.

There's no longer any need for you
To brace yourself
And enter a room full of scary strangers.

Your plastic sword doesn't have to
Behead Hydra for me again and again
From today onward.

The days of holding up a tattered tarp
To protect me from the relentless downpour
Are behind you.

Your frantic heartbeat can slow down.
Your solus
Is finally over.

Coming up with all the right answers
When you didn't know any of the questions
Was cruel, but it's the past.

I'm here now.

The only question that remains is,

Will you forgive me?

Blue

The bright-blue strobe lights
Are pulsing.

I feel the rhythm
Electrify my blood.
I beckon
Its elixir
To flood my body.
I invite the beat
To take over my soul.

I'm gone.

I'm swaying.
I'm moving.
I'm unable to resist
The compulsion
To fall under my spell.

I'm enchanted with me.

All I hear
Is my music.
All I see
Is my luminosity.
All I know that exists
Is my magic.

It's quiet now.

The shadows
Are hurting my eyes.
The stagnant air
Nauseates me.
This Machiavellian solitude
Is strangling me,
Heavy and menacing.

I'm choking.

I fight to escape.

Gasping for air,
I stumble outside,
Seeking the shelter and safety
Of the open sky,
Only to find
A silent patch of
Midnight-blue darkness.

I think I hear myself screaming,
"I want my baby-blue blanket."

The author and her daughter Simrin at Turks and Caicos Islands
Photo: Timothy J. Carlsen

Said a Tree

Said a tree
To the blade of grass,
"Go ahead and grow, little one.
Don't worry about water.
Don't worry about food.
You'll grow by my feet.
You'll grow under my protection."

Said the tree
To the blade of grass,
"Stay close to my trunk
As you learn how to grow.
My roots will be yours.
My shade will shelter you from harm
Till you are one with the soil."

Said the tree
To the blade of grass,
"You are growing up so perfect.
You are a sight to behold.
The leaves on my branches and the birds in the sky
Take delight as you whirl
When the sacred wind blows."

Said the tree
To the blade of grass,
"You are now grown.
You have no worries.

My roots and yours are now anchored
Under the very same ground,
Like the moon and the earth
In worship of each other."

Separate yet connected.

Molasses

Slow down.
You're going too fast.

No,
Keep moving.

Stop right here.
Danger ahead.

Pull out now.
This is as far
As there is to go.

Bursts of flashbulbs,
Flags waving in the air,
Crowds lining up.

I see their lips moving
But can hear no sound—

Words to cheer me up
Or
Messages for me to go home,

I know not.

Bruised, battered, bloodied,

Shuddering,

I hear only one voice.
I move toward its comforting sound.

I see only one light.
I accept its warm invitation.

Assiduously,
Inch by inch,
I move through this black treacle,
Its sticky grip
Loosening with every sigh
And teardrop,

Releasing the antidote
To the poison
Flowing through my broken soul

As I creep
Toward the finish line
Of my unbound sorrow.

Dissolution

The truth doesn't make me happy.
The lies leave me with nothing,

Yet
I battle
To stay in the enchanted forest,
Frantically hoarding the morning dew

As the sun rises.

Scene at a Paris metro station
Photo: Nina S. Carlsen

Carousels and Coffins

I close my eyes,
Wishing away
The desolate landscape
Whizzing by,
But the pariah gray
Refuses to leave me.

I'm scared
Of the mad speed
With which I recklessly twirl myself.

I'm terrified
That I'm going to lose my grip
And fall off the edge.

The calliope
Has taken over the top floor:

Sinister nonstop shrieking,
Steam rising and hissing
Behind the closed doors.

Imprisoned,
I circle
Around the same nothing
Again and again.

I want to get off so bad.

Stop spinning me, please.
Please stop spinning me.
Stop spinning me, please.
Please stop spinning me.

I'm hit hard
By my motionless body.

I'm surprised
By the stillness.

The kind darkness
Gently pries away
My blanket of desperation
Wrapped tightly around my stiff shoulders.

The dignified quiet
Tenderly pulls me into its warm embrace,
Slowly allowing the soft whispers
To receive me and chant,
"Welcome, beautiful darling."

The red velvet caresses me
As I finally settle into your waiting arms.

Dinner Party

The candles stubbornly fight to stay awake,
Their warm glow lazily listening in on conversations
That slowly revealed themselves tonight
Only upon being promised their safety.

The crumpled white napkins lay strewn across the table,
Defiantly ignoring the reproachful looks from the crimson roses.
That are still not ready to give up their decorum
To the intimate ease of the evening.

Half-empty wine glasses
Nestle next to drained coffee cups,
A few random crumbs on the crisp linen
The only hint remaining of the devoured delights.

I hope you'll ignore my unspoken invitation for you to linger.
Just don't say good-bye on your way out.

The author, age eighteen months, in
Lethbridge, Alberta, Canada
Photo: Merriman family album

Look Away

I'm counting on you to look away.

It's the polite thing to do
When you stumble upon me
When I'm feeling
Deep shame.

Shame is a private experience.

Leave me
To have mine.

Don't have me worrying
That you saw me
As I was stripping away
My pain.

I should be able
To dress my wounds
By myself
And on my own.

I'm counting on you to look away.

It's the right thing to do
When you encounter me
Struggling to reach those cuts
That escape my eye.

The contortions,
The twists and the turns,
My revulsion for me
Should have no audience.

I'm counting on you to look away.

It's the proper thing to do
As I thrash
And I flail the mess
That is my broken body
And my starving soul,

Both refusing now
To cover up
My pain and my shame.

I'm hoping you will look away

As I sit,
Disrobed and raw,
Nursing my naked need.

Come Back

Homeless thoughts,
Stranded feelings,
Lost memories

Weigh heavily
In this empty space.

Hollow sounds,
Muffled screams,
Flashback teases,

Unabating torture
In this dark place,

Unanswered questions,
Broken promises,
Wasted love

Float aimlessly
In this lonely vacuum.

I breathe you in
As I ask
My yesterdays
To come back to me.

Debris

The storm
Has now passed,
But
Its fury
Has taken its toll.

The debris
Spreads for miles on end.

The beach
Lies in shocked silence,
Home now
To the washed-up destruction,

The inky sky
A witness
To this ruination,
Grief stricken
In its stillness.

I plead with the dawn,
"Can you wait in the wings
A little bit longer
While I make peace
With this night?"

Call off
Relief and assistance.

Cleanup and rebuild
Can wait.

For now
Just let
The fading darkness
Hold me.

Savor

The word approaches me

Slowly,
Haltingly,
So
It doesn't scare me.

Despite its care and concern,
I'm still frightened as I hear it
Make an entry into my thoughts.

It knows more than I will ever realize
That I never had a voice,

So
It speaks in a whisper
Gently,
Softly,
Trying not to startle me.

But no longer willing to be unheard,

It realizes more than I will ever understand
That I never had a choice.

I struggle
As it quietly continues to make its way into my heart.

I feel it moving through my body.
I shake.
I shudder.
I squirm.

I shut down,

But it refuses to retreat:

Serene,
Strong,
Supporting my trembling breaths

Until I say it.

Stay.

I'm shocked that
After a lifetime of silence,
I can say it out loud.

Stay.

I'm surprised that
After an eternity of being speechless,
I like saying it.

Stay.

I'm filled with jubilation
As I discover
That I can
Savor its sound.

Stay.

Longing

Running toward you
Didn't bring you
Any closer.

It just made me go away.

Driveway

Hidden,
Long,
Secluded,
Winding,
Stately,
Private.

The arborvitaes
Cling
Tightly
To each other:
Tall and fierce,
Proud
Of blocking out the sun
And disallowing the wind
To break through them;

Despotically
Guarding the entrance
To the abode
That remains unseen
From the road
To the occasional traveler
On this unlit stretch
Of endless gravel.

Uninterrupted

Examining
The past
Is never
An easy
Or a
Simple task.

Understanding
The past
When it is
Unknown
Is an
Impossible task.

Dealing
With the past
When it is
Hiding
Is a
Painful task.

Suffering
From a
Buried past
Is an
Ongoing
And
Never-ending task.

Lover

I look in the mirror,
My full concentration
On the last bit
Of preparation
For
A night out
Of fun

And
Whatever else
It may bring my way.

I stare at my lips,
Steadying my hand
As I paint them
Bright red:

A hopefulness,
An anticipation,

A desire
To discover,

A want
To be found.

A final toss of my hair
A dab of my favorite perfume,

And I'm ready
For this night.

I'm eager to see
What's behind the door
Of this honky-tonk.

Who awaits
My attention?

With whom
Will I hold
Nothing back?

I straighten my shoulders.
I take in a deep breath.

I open the door.

I spot him
As soon
As I walk in.

Eyes meet.

An invitation
Is extended.

I decide
I will take my time
To let him know

That I
May have noticed.

I walk past him.

Blasé,

Uninterested,

He follows me,

A smile on his face,
A drink in his hand.

Small talk,
Chitchat,
Crackling energy,
Edgy nervousness,
Sizzling chemistry.

I chide
My beating heart
And sweaty palms
For showing my cards
As I start to rapidly fail
At playing it cool.

He slips in a coin,
Looking to impress me.

Eyebrows raised,

I ask him a question.

I get my answer
In the next second.

Keith's voice
Reaches out
To caress me:

Words of worship

For your body

Or
Mine.

Jukebox
Or him?

I can't seem to
Tell them apart
Any longer.

I'm quickly
Losing myself
To the magic
Of the moment,

Feeling my fantasy
Move slowly
Through every nerve

Of my body.

I can still sense him
And hold him
As he walks away.

I must have said yes
To a drink,

Even though
I don't remember
Saying much.

I'm feeling
Flush,
Warm:

Floating,
Moving,
Dancing
Somewhere else.

Here
It's all getting
A bit
Mixed up.

I'm standing
In front of the board,
A dart in my hand,
Given the advantage

Of going first:

Chivalry,

Overconfidence,

Underestimation.

What's in the assumption
That I need this
Concession?

A
Big
Mistake.

I take my position,

Poised,
Ready,
Confident,

Launching
The dart
In the air.

Bull's-eye.

I cheer for me.

Back and forth,

Thrust after thrust,
The board silently
Taking every
Missile hurled
Its way.

A crowd gathers around us,
Now loudly
Taking sides,
Egging on
Every projectile
Sent its way:
Deadly,
Fierce.

This is
No longer
A
Skirmish.

It's combat.

I'm starting
To feel
Something
In my heart.

I hurl faster.

He keeps up.

I aim for the prize
Again, and again.

The crowd is going crazy.

It's now
A
Frenzy
In here.

I feel the tug
Once again.

I stop.

I tell him,
"Go ahead.
Take a few extra turns.
You may even
Be able
To catch up to me."

"Be my guest
To aim
At the core
Of this board."

I watch
As he throws
Each dart
To win

The game.

As I stand still,
I feel the pain in my heart
Every time I hear the strike.

Bull's-eye.

The crowd goes wild.

He turns around
And looks at me,

Victory in his eyes,
Fist pumped in the air.

The room starts to blur.

The crowd is fading away.

I can't see him anymore.

It's eerily quiet.

All I feel
Is the
Excruciating pain
In my
Heart.

All I see

In my mind
Is the
Assaulted
Dartboard.

All I hear
Are the
Anguished cries
Coming from
Inside me.

I now get it.

I now see it.

I now understand it:

The ugliness,
The violence,
The sordidness
Of what I have done to you.

I can't bear it.

I arranged the assault.
I made the call for cruelty.
I threw the punishment party.

I unlocked the door to deprave you.
I stocked the tools of torture.
I cast the first stone.

I cheered on the vicious crowd
As they hurled daggers at you.

I tuned out
Your voice
When it was
Powerful
And
Strong
And
Honest.

I authorized
Any sound
Coming from
You
To be turned
Off.

I
Mercilessly
Sanctioned you
When you
Dared
To ask
Why.

After a while
The only
Sounds
Heard

Were the
Sinister cheers
And jeers
From the
Rabid
Crowd
Around
You.

Your
Anguished
Cries
For help
Were
First
Drowned out
By that noise,

Then
No
Longer
Heard.

I
Was the one
Who
Forbade you
To speak,

Rendering
You

Helpless
and
Mute,

Egging them on
To hurl
Pain
Upon
You.

I gave truth
To their lies.

I listened
To you last.

I can't bear my shame.

I wrap myself
Around
You.

I Cover
You
Up.

I
Shield
You.

I drape

You
Like a
Towering
Weeping Willow
In a
Quiet,
Shady
Meadow.

I hide you
In my
Tender embrace.

I want to come
Back to you
Every
Second of
The moment.

I want to hear your
Thoughts
Before
You think
Them.

I hunger
To feel
You
When apart from
You.

I long
To return to you
When
Away from
You.

I dream
Of
Making
You
Smile.

I promise
To
Shelter
You
From harm.

I
Live
To
Restore
You.

The room
Comes back into focus.

I can clearly hear
The claptrap
Coming from the
Insipid crowd.

I see his common-day face.

I take down the
Beautifully mangled board.

I leave with
My
Lover.

I walk out
With
Me.

The Fan

As I lay under you,
I see
White,

Virginal and uncomplicated,
Fresh,
Spotless,
Clean:

A welcome sight
Away
From the killing fields.

Even with my eyes closed,
I can picture you
Moving
Against the clock,
Blowing puffs
Of cool air
Straight down
To my troubled brow.

Then subtly,
Unostentatiously,
Reading me,
Changing course
Without skipping a beat,
Reversing now

To warm me up,
Pulling
The frozen air from around my stiff body
Up
Next to you.

I need to slow my heartbeat down
To match your steady drone.
I have to shush my burning brain
So I may catch what you have to say.

Only when I'm still
Can I hear:

I've got you.

A Hard Conversation

I'm not here
To make it
Easy for you.

I'm here to
To make it
True for me.

It's time
For me to know
That you see
Me.

You don't have to.

It's really
Your
Choice.

But understand
That I won't be waiting here
For you to
Know me.

I know myself.
That's good enough for me.

You and Me

It's an ongoing conversation,
Not a guarantee.

Boulder

I stripped
All
That I wore
And
All
That still covered me.
How did you get to stay?
Forcibly taking over
My begrudging breasts,
A trespasser
Gone rogue,
Viciously
Crushing my heart,
Perfidiously
Suffocating my mind,
Unlawfully
Laying claim
To my timid breaths
And my tender thoughts.

One of the 177 canals in Venice, Italy
Photo: Timothy J. Carlsen

Venetian Ball

Vesper:

Earnest incantations,
Ceremonious
In synchronized harmony,
Gentle ripples
That quietly glisten
Over the shimmery cover
Of the crisscrossing ribbons,
Respectfully darkening
In homage
To the regal retreat
Of the golden light.

Reverberations
Of the sweet, holy words
Of gratitude and confession
Rise solemnly,
Carried by the wings
Of the thick mist
That suffuses the sky
With a pious mystery.

The sound trespasses
Through the open windows
Of the palazzo,

Boldly

Finding me,

Openly
Encompassing me,

Assertively
Entering me,

Comfortably
Occupying me,

Unapologetically
Filling me

Straight
Through my awaiting ears,

Deep
Into my starved soul.

This litany
Comes in,
Accompanied by
Sweet messages
From blush roses in the garden,
Becoming one
With the fragrance
Of the jasmine oil
That rises from my skin.

The celestial chants

Watch in reverential silence
As I invite
The red velvet to
Touch me,
Permitting its softness
To wrap me
In quiet worship.
They silently gasp
At the brilliance
Of the jewels
That I allow
To adorn me.
They can barely
Keep their composure
As I take my mask
To my naked face.

Now
Hidden and unrevealed,
Anonymous and unknown,
I glide over the water
Into the rapture of the night:

Announcements and introductions,
Receiving lines and winding staircases,
Illuminated ballrooms and quiet libraries
Dark corners and welcoming balconies,
Shining candelabras and cascading flowers,
Brocade draperies and silk tablecloths,
Masks and waltzes,
Violins, violas, and cellos,

Memories and coverups.

The room takes a spin and dips.

Suddenly,
Sweat travels down my spine,
Yet I shiver.

The heat rises to the ceiling,
Even though a cold chill
Starts to settle in my bones.
The tantalizing conversations
Are now sounding tepid to me.
The divine crowd
Is quickly resembling debauchery
To my awakening mind.

My glow is turning
Brassy and brittle.
My bedazzling ball gown,
Hiding a lifetime of sins
I committed against myself,
Is now closing in on me.
My exquisite silk corset
Sucks the air out of my lungs,
Strangling me
While delicacy and gentleness
Exit the room without
A backward glance.

A harsh breeze fans

The suffocation rising in my
Rapidly constricting throat.

I'm overcome by the fumes
Of my fake finery.

I've tried my hardest to resist
Falling in love with me,
Wasting all my waking moments,
Stubbornly
Refusing to be lured
By my irresistible draw,
Something
So easy and natural
To fall into
Turning into
A long, drawn-out,
Ferocious battle
Of staying away.

I've done my damnedest to
Turn my face away from my smile
Time after time,
Reaching to dim the light within
Whenever it dared to shine,
Cruelly walking away from me
While clandestinely longing
To be one with me
In my secret dreams.

As I thoughtlessly lay

With the cacophonous wind,
I forgot
How good it felt
To be held by me.

I played this wicked game
So many times
That it became a heartache
That was familiar
And easy to bear,

Finally
Becoming a ruin
I couldn't live without.

I stop.

I strip.

I
Look
At
Me.

An ethereal reality sets in.

I own every throb
That pierces my heart.
I lay claim to every thrill
That pulses in my veins.
I unabashedly bathe

In the rapture of my pleasure.
I proudly display every scar
That calls my body home.

I say,

"Look
All you want
At my unsightly nakedness.

Stare.

Gawk."

I'm proud
To call this mangled body mine.
I worship my deformities.
I live in the ecstasy
Of this celebration
Of my grotesquerie.

My glory blazes my world.
My flames torch my sky.

The cold air can't touch me.

I'm wrapped up in my own heat.

It's warm
Like the finest cashmere
Woven by beautiful

Bent-over bodies
Hidden and forgotten
In the backstreets of this city,
Toiling through the night
With swollen and stiff fingers,
Stubbornly working through the pain,
Refusing to surrender
To their agony,
Rebelling against the torture
Of the ravages of time,
Never getting to see
Who they cover,
Who they protect,
Who they release,
Who they cloak
With their devotion
To the labor of their love.

Look at how the fervor
Of this invisible sheath they made
Cocoons me.
Feel how tenderly it
Wraps me,

No longer unknown,
Unwilling
To be forced to be concealed
Like
A dirty secret.

I revel in the feel of its softness.
I experience its indulgent fineness.
I willingly surrender to its seduction.
I invite its decadent luxury to corrupt me.

As desire floods my body,
My aching breasts
And my quivering womb
Light the fire raging in me.

I burn myself alive
With this inferno
Fueled by the sparks
Flying through me
That instantly combust
When they touch the want
That deluges my body.

I dance
In the rainfall
Of my delight,
Washed and renewed,
Reborn,
Alive.

I'm lit.
I'm aglow.
I'm irresistible.

I'm untouchable.

This pedestal is mine.

I built it.

It is indestructible

Just like me.

I stand in the center of this room.

You can look at me.
You can laugh at me.
You can love me.
You can covet me.
You can hate me.
You can ignore me.
You can talk about me.
You can think you read me.
You can imagine me.
You can fail me.
You can hurt me.
You can guess me.
You can betray me.
You can want me.
You can judge me.

You can walk away from me,

But you can't touch me.

My cracks are perfect.
My exile is my home.
My suffering is my insight.
My confusion is my clarity.
My agony is my voice.
My survival is my celebration.
My quietus is my birth.

My mask is off,

Such sweet relief.

My ugliness is unveiled.

There is nothing left to reveal.

My beauty is simple.
My grace is vast.
My love is unending.

Nightfall

At the end of the day,
All I get to keep
Is
The love
I gave away.

Sunshine

I
Don't look
For
My happiness
From
Anyone.

I
Don't owe
My happiness
To
Anyone.

It's mine
To
Find.

It's mine
To
Keep.

Proof

I am not a frightened whisper.
I am a loud voice.
I am not the ghost of an apparition.
I am a rock.
I am not floating in a vacuum.
I have roots.

My past
Is
No longer
My
Perpetual present.

Nor
Is it
My
Predictable future.

I hear
Me.

I see
Me.

I feel
Me.

Repair

I want to live truthfully
I want to live my truth

I want to live fully
I want to feel full

I want to live joyfully
I want to spread joy

I want to be
Sublimely in love with you

I want to live
Always in love with me

The author at home in Edison, New Jersey, USA
Photo: Timothy J. Carlsen

Sovereign

Loving myself set me free to love others.
Being loved by someone set me free to love myself-

Loving myself allowed me to forgive you for not loving me.
Being loved by someone allowed me to forget that you didn't
love me-

Loving myself released me from my need to have you love me.
Being loved by someone connected me to my need to love me-

Love set me free.

Epilogue

1. Depression and Anxiety

According to the World Health Organization (WHO),

- depression is a common mental disorder;
- depression is the leading cause of disability worldwide, and it is a major contributor to the overall global burden of disease;
- more women are affected by depression than men;
- at its worst, depression can lead to suicide;
- there are effective treatments for depression.

Depression is treatable, with talking therapies or antidepressant medication or a combination of these.

The burden of depression and other mental health conditions is on the rise globally. "More than 300 million people are now living with depression, an increase of more than 18% between 2005 and 2015."[1]

For more information, see WHO publication number WHO/MSD/MER/2017.2 titled "Depression and Other Common Mental Disorders—Global Health Estimates."

The National Institute of Mental Health (NIMH) states the following as of 2016: "An estimated 3.1 million adolescents aged 12 to 17 in the United States had at least one major depressive

---

[1] "Depression: let's talk", World Health Organization, accessed February 25, 2018 http://www.who.int/mental_health/management/depression/en/

episode. This number represented 12.8% of the U.S. population aged 12 to 17."[2]

The WHO has identified strong links between depression and other noncommunicable disorders and diseases. Depression increases the risk of substance use disorders and diseases such as diabetes and heart disease. The opposite is also true; people with these other conditions have a higher risk of depression.

Depression is also an important risk factor for suicide, which claims hundreds of thousands of lives each year. Depression is a common mental illness characterized by persistent sadness and a loss of interest in activities people normally enjoy, accompanied by an inability to carry out daily activities, for fourteen days or longer.

In addition, people suffering from depression normally have several of the following: a loss of energy; a change in appetite; a problem with sleeping more or less; anxiety; reduced concentration; indecisiveness; restlessness; feelings of worthlessness, guilt, or hopelessness; and thoughts of self-harm or suicide.

You can help fight this epidemic by learning more about depression. Further, talking openly and proactively about depression lessens the burden of shame and silence that sufferers feel, shame that prevents them from seeking the help and support they need.

2. Adverse Childhood Experiences (ACEs)

---

[2] "Prevalence of Major Depressive Episode Among Adolescents", National Institute of Mental Health, accessed February 25, 2018, https://www. nimh.nih.gov/health/statistics/major-depression.shtml

According to the Centers for Disease Control and Prevention (CDC), childhood experiences, both positive and negative, have a tremendous impact on future violence victimization and perpetration, and lifelong health and opportunity. As such, early experiences are an important public health issue. Much of the foundational research in this area has been referred to as Adverse Childhood Experiences (ACEs).

ACEs can be prevented.

You can learn more about preventing ACEs in your community by visiting the CDC website (https://www.cdc.gov/violenceprevention/acestudy/about.html).

3. Trauma and the Brain

The human brain is a social organ. We are physiologically and neurobiologically designed to connect with others. We are born to love and form relationships with others. Trauma can result in brain damage that, among many other negative consequences, also makes it hard for an affected individual to pursue or maintain loving relationships.

Research on trauma and its effects on the developing brain and mind is ongoing. You can learn more by visiting these websites:

Childtrauma.org

Traumacenter.org

Mindsightinstitute.com

4. Sleep and Mental Health

Does sleep deprivation cause depression and mood disorders or vice versa? Research shows that there may be a bidirectional relationship between the two. There is a wealth of ongoing research dedicated to understanding the relationship between sleep health and wellness, in addition to understanding the physical effects of sleep deprivation on our brains and bodies.

The Golden Bear Sleep and Mood Research Clinic at the University of California in Berkley, California, is dedicated to improving treatments for insomnia and other sleep disturbances as well as bipolar disorder and depression in teenagers and adults. You can learn more about the work being done there by visiting their website (https://www.ocf.berkeley.edu/~ahsleep).

5. Above All Else

Anam Cara is an Irish phrase that loosely translates as "soul mate." *Anam* is the Gaelic word for "soul," and *Cara* is the word for "friend."

Above all, we are healed when another human being gifts us with his or her presence, compassion, and empathy while hearing our story of suffering without judgment.

We heal when we feel seen.

It is the relationship that heals.

About the Author

Dr. Sunita Merriman is a graduate of New York University, College of Dentistry; and the founder of the New Jersey Dental Sleep Medicine Center in Westfield, New Jersey. For over twenty years, she has been dedicated to treating her patients with the belief that the mind, body, and soul are connected.

Stripping: My Fight to Find Me is her first published book. She is currently working on her second book, *Permission: To Live as Me*, which is a compilation of inspiring stories of individuals who overcame seemingly impossible obstacles to find their true selves and live lives of their design.

Dr. Merriman lives in Edison, New Jersey, with her husband and their two daughters.

Dr. Merriman is dedicated to bringing attention to the importance of mind health and sleep as the fundamental pillars of our existence and to sharing and promoting her belief in the infinite potential of the human spirit.

To learn more about Dr. Sunita Merriman, visit
sunitamerriman.com

To read Sunita's journal. visit
selfloveselfcarefirst.com/

You can also connect with Sunita here:
linkedin.com/in/dr-sunita-merriman-87b86416/
facebook.com/sunitamerrimanpoetry
instagram.com/sunitapoetry
twitter.com/sunitapoetry
Search Dr. Sunita Merriman on YouTube

You are invited to
#jointhemovement
#selfloveselfcarefirst

From Sunita Merriman's next book, Permission: To Live as Me

Ijaazat*

I haven't lived yet.
I have just had a life.

Ijaazat
Origin: Arabic
Ijaazat is an Urdu word meaning "permission/sanctioned."